IMAGES
of America

SLATER MILL

IMAGES
of America

SLATER MILL

Sarah Leavitt
Slater Mill Historic Site

ARCADIA

First published 1997
Copyright © Sarah Leavitt, Slater Mill Historic Site, 1997

ISBN 0-7524-0567-5

Published by Arcadia Publishing,
an imprint of the Chalford Publishing Corporation
One Washington Center, Dover, New Hampshire 03820
Printed in Great Britain

Library of Congress Cataloging-in-Publication Data applied for

Contents

Acknowledgments   6

Introduction   7

1.   Samuel Slater: Life and Legend   11

2.   Crinolines, Coffin Trimmings, and Cycles   25

3.   Restoration and Quiet Times   45

4.   Museum and Community Center   61

5.   Urban Renewal and Site Expansion   81

Acknowledgments

Special thanks to the staff of Slater Mill Historic Site: Gloria Abysalh, Karin Conopask, Louis Hutchins, Gail Fowler Mohanty, Laura Raff, Marsha Schlesinger and Jeanne Zavada.

Unless otherwise noted, photographs are from the collection of Slater Mill Historic Site.

This project was funded in part by the Blackstone River Valley National Heritage Corridor Commission.

Introduction

SLATER MILL HISTORIC SITE

Slater Mill Historic Site is a complex of three historic buildings on the banks of the Blackstone River in Pawtucket, Rhode Island. The museum interprets the history of the industrial revolution, from the manufacture of textiles by hand to factory production, and includes an operative machine shop. Slater Mill has a long history, having witnessed the transition of Pawtucket's economy from agriculture to industry and then to urban renewal and tourism. This book highlights the changes in the building over time, and traces the different meanings of the historic structure.

SAMUEL SLATER: LIFE AND LEGEND

Samuel Slater, born in 1768 in Belper, England, was apprenticed in Jedediah Strutt's spinning mills and was familiar with the water-powered cotton manufacture of the English industrial revolution. Despite laws forbidding textile workers from emigrating, Slater decided to look for a new market for his skills and left for America in 1789. He arrived in New York but was soon directed to Providence, where he was offered a partnership by Smith Brown (nephew of merchant Moses Brown) and William Almy (Moses Brown's son-in-law) if he could help them build the necessary cotton machines to start their factory. Moses Brown had been working to establish cotton manufacturing in Rhode Island since 1787 but could not spin cotton strong enough to warp a loom. He needed Slater's help. For most of 1790, the new firm of Almy, Brown, and Slater worked on their machinery. Their first enterprise, housed in Ezekiel Carpenter's clothier's shop, employed twelve children and began spinning cotton on December 20, 1790.

Workshops and small mills used the powerful Blackstone River to operate their machinery well before Samuel Slater arrived in Pawtucket. The village economy had already begun its evolution from agriculture to industry. With single-process mills and forges clustered around the waterfalls, Pawtucket was poised for industry on a larger scale. The Blackstone River would provide the energy for hundreds of mills in the nineteenth century.

The shop where Slater first operated his new machinery was soon too small for the growing enterprise. In 1792, to prepare for their larger facility, Almy, Brown, and Slater constructed a dam above Pawtucket Falls on the Blackstone River. The new mill they built in 1793 to house their operation still stands today.

Almy, Brown, and Slater continued to spin cotton at their 1793 mill in Pawtucket for about three decades, although they owned many other mills. In 1801 they expanded the first mill 57 feet to the north. The production capacity of the mill stayed the same for many years after this addition. In 1820, the *Manufacturers Census for Massachusetts and Rhode Island* noted that the mill employed thirteen men, five women, and fifty-two children spinning yarn from Sea Island and Upland cotton. The mill housed about fifteen hundred spindles, which was an impressive number in the early nineteenth century but would soon seem small in comparison to the capacity of the newer mills.

During the first few decades of the industrial revolution in New England, the cotton mills were small and appeared on the banks of the many regional rivers and streams. The weaving was done outside the mill in workers' homes on hand looms. During the series of embargoes initiated in 1807 and through the War of 1812, American textile manufacturers avoided competition from the more established British mills, and factory towns grew all over New England. Slater's enterprise began a long, slow process that continued to expand throughout the nineteenth century, especially in cities like Lowell and Fall River, Massachusetts.

Partly due to financial trouble and disagreements with his partners, Slater sold his shares in the "old mill" during the depression of 1829. However, Almy and Brown continued to spin cotton in Pawtucket. Several additions to the building expanded its production, and by 1832 the mill had looms as well as spinning frames. Despite these improvements, mill complexes such as those located in Lowell, Massachusetts, surpassed Pawtucket's in size by the end of the 1820s.

CRINOLINES, COFFIN TRIMMINGS, AND CYCLES

Major changes took place at Slater Mill during the 1840s and 1850s. The remaining heirs of the original owners, Almy and William Jenkins, sold the mill building to another firm. The next few owners rented space in the mill to other businesses. In the first few decades of the post-Almy and Brown years, the building continued to house textile production. Spinning and weaving companies run by Gideon Smith and H. Jerauld operated in the mill for a decade between 1846 and 1865. Jerauld, who had financial troubles, rented out the building to one of the more successful businesses housed there in its long history, the Pawtucket Hair Cloth Company. Despite periods of prosperity, the middle decades of the century ended with near-silence from the mill during the Civil War.

Fortunately for the survival of the landmark, the "old mill" was bought by the enterprising firm of Pratt and Spencer in 1865. This company made several improvements to the building and replaced the water wheels with more efficient turbines. Also, raising the entire building up by 2 feet enabled the mill to house larger textile machinery. The variety and number of businesses moving in and out of Slater Mill over the next six decades was staggering. Crinolines, straw bonnets, coffin trimmings, jewelers' tools, and bicycles represent only part of the building's production output from the late nineteenth century.

The early twentieth century was the final productive time for the Old Slater Mill. Many sheds for storage and extra facilities had been built around the site. The building itself was almost unrecognizable from its original form, since the oldest part of the building had been completely surrounded by newer structures and additions. The area around the mill had built up as well, with workers' housing, machine shops, dye works, and other mills crowded in around the banks of the Blackstone. Buildings reached down to the water on both sides of the river. Although much of the textile industry had by this time moved away from New England, the industrial economy remained. The building boom of the prosperous textile years meant that new businesses could move right into the city's many mills, and benefit from what already existed. The Slater Mill building was still unique among the other buildings because of its wood construction and, of course, its history. The mill would thereafter stand as a shrine.

RESTORATION AND QUIET TIMES

Historic preservation in the 1920s was generally a movement to save monuments and structures related to United States military or government personnel. Large money-making campaigns and restoration projects had never been started to save an industrial site. Most preservationists, such as the Daughters of the American Revolution, did a remarkable job of saving birthplaces and family homesteads, but did not make an effort to save factory buildings. When the owner of the Old Slater Mill, Job Spencer, died in 1920, his estate put the building up for sale. Textile executives in Pawtucket, eager to save a landmark of their industry, recognized their opportunity. At a 1921 meeting at the To Kalon Club in Pawtucket, local textile leaders formed the Old Slater Mill Association, whose goal was to raise money for the preservation of the mill. Early supporters included members of the local textile production community and Samuel Slater's descendants, most prominently his grandson's wife, Mabel Slater, who donated $25,000.

Perhaps because of the unusual nature of the preservation attempt, and the great sums of money needed to remove additions to the building and other structures around the site, the transformation from factory to museum was gradual. Several businesses, such as the Moncrief Machine Company, still ran their operations from the mill and had to leave. The restoration project began in 1924, and included the removal of outbuildings and additions. The association decided to return the mill to its c. 1835 appearance, removing many of the additions but keeping the wings that extended out from the original structure. They also kept the raised brick foundation. The removal of one hundred years of building fabric and the subsequent landscaping of the grounds helped to transform this area of industrial decline into a tourist attraction.

The decades after the restoration were disappointing for the Old Slater Mill Association because the museum did not have enough money to open full time. Instead, the mill sponsored a trade show in the 1930s and opened the doors to the public for special events. The Great Depression hit Pawtucket's textile industry hard, closing or downsizing many of the remaining businesses. This was not a good time to raise money, but the association certainly tried. Henry Dexter, the first president and member of the association, traveled to cotton conventions all over the country to gain support for the museum. The exclusive function of the association at this time was fund-raising, and little attention was given to creating exhibitions inside the old mill. In fact, many members of the board wanted to preserve the mill itself as a monument, not necessarily allowing the public inside. The Old Slater Mill stood during this period as a quiet landmark of Pawtucket's early industrial glory.

THE NEW MUSEUM AS COMMUNITY CENTER

In 1949 the restored mill was painted red with white trim, a color scheme approved by local preservationists as appropriate for a New England historical building. The old mill now stood almost alone on the river bank, bereft of its supporting buildings and industries, no longer surrounded by other factories. In effect, by separating the mill from its industrial environment, the association had changed the landscape into a park and the mill into a comforting community center. Pawtucket business executives had made history by preserving an industrial site, but they did not preserve the industrial setting.

Horatio Nelson Slater, Samuel's great-grandson, was an early supporter of the museum and paid the salary for the first curator—Daniel Tower—beginning in 1952. In the 1950s, Tower and the next director, Donald Shepard, spent the bulk of their time campaigning for financial support from the dying textile industry in both New England and the South. With the Slater family distancing themselves throughout this decade, citing differences in opinion about the mission of the mill, board members and staff struggled to keep the museum open. They saw the building as a liaison between the industrial history of Pawtucket and the modern city.

Machines, models, craft tools, and memorabilia continued to be donated to the mill in the 1950s, and they became part of a permanent display on the museum's first floor. Visitors to the mill learned about the accomplishments of Samuel Slater and about the significance of some early machines.

The outreach program in the 1960s brought dozens of varied exhibits to the site. Betty Johnson, a lifelong Pawtucket resident who worked at the mill as the exhibit coordinator, focused the special exhibits on popular subjects to get more and more visitors into the mill. Tropical fish and Lafayette china, among other collections, brought new people. The involvement of the Junior Women's Club, the Pawtucket Garden Club, and the Stamp Club helped to generate interest. Timely exhibits, such as one on Civil Defense in 1962, helped the museum become a part of peoples' lives. Local Girl Scouts served as tour guides, and beauty pageant winners posed on the site in cotton dresses. The successful museum store on the second floor sold napkins and place mats that were hand-woven during public demonstrations.

URBAN RENEWAL AND SITE EXPANSION

Urban renewal transformed downtown Pawtucket in the 1960s. This federally funded national program redesigned dozens of cities, forcing the destruction of nineteenth-century architecture in favor of a modernized vision of the American city. Instead of preserving old structures, neighborhoods, and historic districts, as others had done in Providence, the Slater Renewal Project in downtown Pawtucket funded the destruction of entire city blocks. The sterile reconstruction of the area signaled the end of an era for Pawtucket.

City planners had the idea, as part of an urban renewal concept in 1963, to build an industrial history village in downtown Pawtucket. Surviving old houses in the area would be converted into craft and antique stores, and "Mill Village" would sell decorative wallpapers and textiles designated as Pawtucket Patterns. Because nineteenth-century houses and mills remained in the area, this was a feasible plan, but it was abandoned for lack of money. The houses have since been demolished.

The Sylvanus Brown House and Wilkinson Mill were added to the museum complex in the 1970s and '80s. Extensive research into the history of each building created different museum environments. Samuel Slater and his mythical memory had been a significant part of the mill's story in the 1950s and '60s. However, beginning in the 1970s, tour guides discussed mill strikes in Pawtucket, child labor laws, and the social stratification of the work force. New directors Paul Rivard and Patrick Malone emphasized current scholarship on technology and social history, ending the once-popular exhibits on non-textile subjects. The opening of the 1758 Brown House created a space to demonstrate hand spinning and weaving, and fiber arts classes promoted the public interest in handicrafts. For the industrial component, archaeologists researched the wheel pit in the Wilkinson Mill and brought water power back to operate the machinery in the shop.

In the Slater Mill, tourists and students learn the history of textiles, technology, and water power. Annual festivals and visits from local, state, and national politicians—all eager to use the historic mill as a backdrop—help bring the community to the site. Programs and preservation efforts at the Slater Mill contribute to the rejuvenation of Pawtucket and the entire region, and the site is an active supporter of new projects including the Blackstone Tourism Council's Visitor Center and the Blackstone River Valley National Heritage Corridor, a cooperative effort between privately owned natural and historic sites and the National Park Service. The Old Slater Mill has stood on the same site since 1793, playing an important role in Pawtucket by both making and teaching history.

One

Samuel Slater: Life and Legend

Images in this chapter include paintings, drawings, and objects that are part of the collection of Slater Mill Historic Site. The machines, landscapes, buildings, and people pictured here contributed to Samuel Slater's success.

Slater lived and worked in many cities, from Belper, England, to Pawtucket and Slatersville, Rhode Island, to Webster, Massachusetts, where he died in 1835. The mill in Pawtucket was his first, and most historically significant, building. Despite his successes elsewhere, Slater developed his most original innovations in Pawtucket.

The Cotton Centennial of 1890 marked an important moment in the history of textile production in Pawtucket, since at that point the industry could still celebrate activity instead of forecasting disaster. By honoring Samuel Slater, the planners of the celebration ensured his lasting memory in the annals of industrial history, but more especially in the local history of Pawtucket. Some of the same business leaders who marched in the parade that year would agitate to rescue the Slater Mill only decades later.

This portrait demonstrates the prestige Samuel Slater attained as a successful industrialist. According to one of Slater's biographers, he was worth over ten million dollars by the time of his death in 1835. He had built a flourishing empire of spinning mills all over northern Rhode Island and southern Massachusetts. (Courtesy of Pawtucket Public Library.)

Brought up in the English cotton-manufacturing town of Belper (pictured here), Samuel Slater apprenticed at a spinning mill. There he learned about the new water-powered technology invented by Richard Arkwright in the 1760s. English manufacturing cities preceded those in America by several decades.

Holly House, Samuel Slater's birthplace in England, gets its name from the trees growing around the site. The establishment of the Slater Mill museum helped build interest in the history of this famous Rhode Islander, leading people on journeys back to England to see his ancestral home.

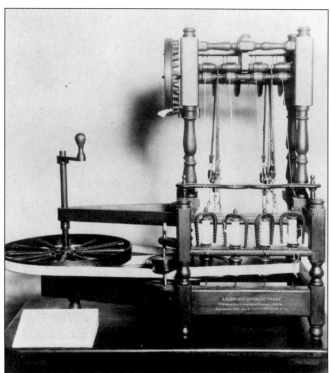

Richard Arkwright was the first to develop water-powered cotton-spinning machinery. This is a model of his spinning frame, which stretched out the cotton and twisted the strands together. Samuel Slater learned how to operate these machines and would later recreate them in Pawtucket.

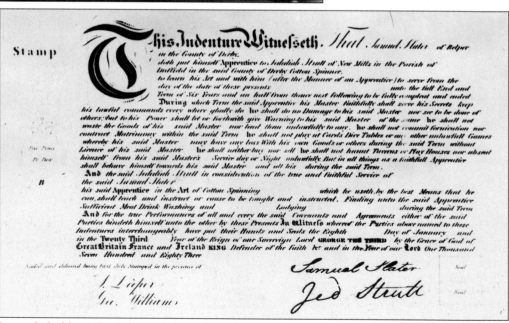

Laws forbidding English textile workers from emigrating seem not to have been strictly enforced, since Samuel Slater actually carried his indenture papers with him to prove to his future employers that he was qualified. Slater's escape from England was a planned attempt to open the cotton-spinning industry in America.

Pawtucket, the Algonquin name for "falling water," was located on a major route between Boston and Providence. The city would grow in industrial importance over the eighteenth century, as forecast in the urbanization beyond the bridge in this engraving. Skilled artisans set up shop in the town in part because of access to the water power that eventually attracted Samuel Slater and the early cotton industry.

Moses Brown was a member of one of Providence's most successful families. As a Quaker, he had resisted his brothers' involvement in the slave trade; however, by financing Slater's spinning mill he made his enterprise dependent on the South's plantation economy. He hoped the new mill would provide jobs for women and children, traditionally under-employed groups.

An extant plastering bill determined the measurements for this drawing of Almy, Brown, and Slater's mill. In 1793, Benjamin Kingsley was hired to plaster the new factory, a small 43-by-29-foot structure with 28 windows and 2 1/2 stories. Most likely, Slater Mill was plastered and painted to help protect the wood from fire and to allow light to reflect.

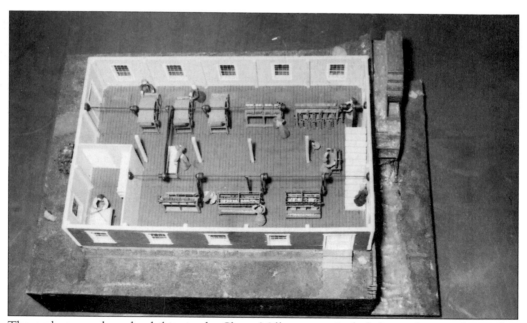

The early research and exhibits in the Slater Mill museum included speculations about what the original Almy, Brown, and Slater operation had looked like. This model, built by Edward Jaysanne in 1952, was based on evidence that the mill contained several carding and spinning machines, and little else.

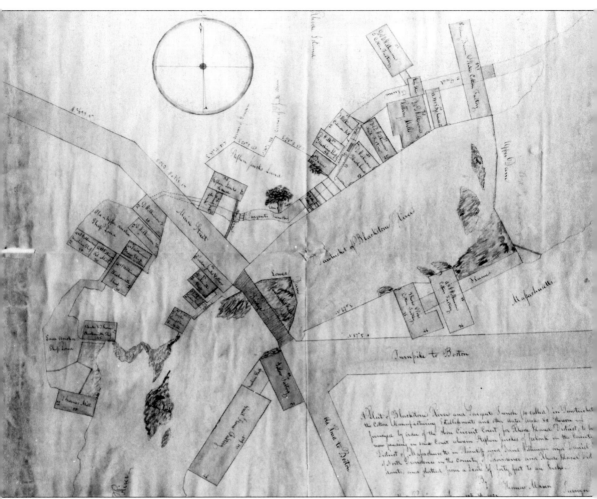

This map, depicting the area around the "Almy, Brown & Slater Cotton Factory" about 1800, was drawn as part of Thomas Mann's deposition of 1823 concerning water rights in Pawtucket. Because of the impressive power generated by the Blackstone River, the site attracted many mills and forges. In 1826, Judge Story granted specific water rights to certain lots of land and landowners. His opinion stands today as a guide to water rights and uses along the Blackstone in Pawtucket.

Slater and his partners had trouble building this carding machine, and turned to artisan Pliney Earle to help them. Although Slater had worked with machines like this in Belper, he needed the assistance of many American artisans to recreate the technology. Slater's carding machine of 1790 is presently in the collection of the Smithsonian Institution in Washington, D.C. (Courtesy of the Smithsonian Institution.)

The *Progress of Cotton*, a series of drawings depicting the various stages in cotton production, was found in the Slater Mill during the restoration of the building in the 1920s. This image depicts the carders, machines made up of leather-covered rollers fixed with metal pins that comb the cotton fibers into parallel lines.

Samuel Slater's cotton-spinning frame was quite similar to those he had worked with in England. Machines like this one would spin white cotton yarn in his mill, which would be taken to out-workers who would warp their looms and weave plain cotton sheeting and shirting. This photograph shows the frame on display at the Cotton Centennial in 1890.

This image depicts a spinning room at a larger operation than the one Almy, Brown, and Slater had in Pawtucket, but it shows cotton spinning at work. Shown here is mule spinning, a technology introduced into Almy, Brown, and Slater's mill in 1804.

David Wilkinson operated a machine shop on the first floor of his 1810 mill, while his father, Oziel Wilkinson, ran a spinning and weaving mill on the upper floors. David helped build many of Slater's machines, and his shop was a site of innovation on the part of local machinists. Despite much early success, the Wilkinsons' business failed during the bank crisis of 1829. (Courtesy of Lewis Cole.)

Once Samuel Slater was established in New England as an industrialist, he asked his brother John to come and help him with a new venture. The two Slaters founded a company town, Slatersville, in northern Rhode Island. In Slatersville, John and Samuel Slater fostered the development of the power loom by hiring inventor William Gilmore.

This photograph shows the interior of one of the mill buildings in Slatersville. The weave room is similar to many other mill interiors, with the leather belting attached to the line shafting, and probably a water wheel or turbine. Although Almy, Brown, and Slater only carded and spun cotton at their mill in Pawtucket, Slater did include weaving in some of his new enterprises.

Young workers at a Slatersville mill stand outside their factory and pose for a photograph in the late nineteenth century. Control of Slater & Sons had passed to Samuel's son Horatio Nelson, who continued to expand the company. The mill village of Slatersville, established in 1806, still retains the built environment of its textile years.

These men made up the Cotton Centennial Committee, which coordinated the largest display of civic pride Pawtucket had ever seen. They planned an entire week of events to celebrate the one hundred years since Samuel Slater had opened his first mill. As prominent business leaders, these men were justly proud of their industrial city.

With images of Samuel Slater and his mill, this apron's red, white, and blue fabric links patriotism to Pawtucket's industrial hero. The apron was produced by the Dunnell Manufacturing Company for the Cotton Centennial in 1890. Pawtucket's New Idea store, specializing in fancy aprons, designed the pattern. A Pawtucket woman may have worn this apron in one of the many parades during the week-long festival.

Samuel Slater's picture rose high above Broad Street during the Cotton Centennial Celebration of 1890. The city-wide festival commemorated Slater's first cotton mill, and Slater was the recognized hero of the day. Images of his mill and his Sunday school, said to be the first in the country, decorated the city, as parades of military groups and schoolchildren marched through the streets.

Recognition of the importance of Slater Mill resulted in the celebration of the structure during the city-wide Cotton Centennial Celebration of 1890. The mill, along with Samuel Slater's picture, birthplace, and home, were featured on dozens of items such as this kerchief. Pawtucket's business economy had diversified, but cotton was still the symbol of the city's rise to industrial prominence.

Samuel Slater's first house in Pawtucket was modest, but his later home was termed a "mansion." This drawing is from the Cotton Centennial Program of 1890, when Slater was already a legend. He had many homes in Rhode Island: one on Benefit Street in Providence was temporarily used as a dormitory for students at Pembroke College at the beginning of the twentieth century.

This bank bill illustrates Slater's importance to Pawtucket. During the nineteenth century, the name "Slater" was attached to many municipal services, including the bank. The image of the loom on the bank bill indicates the symbolism of his name and its relation to the textile industry.

Two
Crinolines, Coffin Trimmings, and Cycles

Between 1870 and 1924, the Old Slater Mill was the subject of dozens of photographs and artistic works. As an icon of Pawtucket's history and as a busy factory, the site attracted photographers and amateur painters alike. These images help document changes in the ownership of the building as well as structural alterations.

While Slater Mill housed businesses selling everything from ring travelers to automobiles, the industrial landscape of Pawtucket grew up around it. This chapter documents a city of factories which is impossible to see now, especially in the downtown area. Together, the photographs create a visual record of the most prosperous years of industrial Pawtucket.

The images in this section illustrate the strength of the symbolism of the legendary life and work of Samuel Slater for the city of Pawtucket. As a building changes to suit its new ownership or purpose, its prior history is often forgotten. Despite all the changes to the Old Slater Mill, however, it never lost its identity. The building was Pawtucket's link to its industrial past, an icon of historical dominance even in the face of economic failure.

This woodcut shows the Old Slater Mill about 1840. Copied from a painting, the image was reproduced in the Cotton Centennial book of 1890. Although the drawing shows men fishing in the foreground, the pollution of the Blackstone River by 1840 had already killed off most of the fish.

A low addition had been built into the side of one of the wings at Slater Mill by the time of this drawing, incorrectly dated but likely from 1850. In later years, new businesses demanding more room would build second and third floors on that addition, which would eventually be taken down in 1924.

In the 1870s, buildings were packed in from Mill Street all the way to the river. Among these were perhaps a company store, a picker house to prepare the cotton for carding and spinning machinery, and other cotton mills or bleacheries. The two buildings to the left of Slater Mill extend over the water's edge, supported by columns.

Job L. Spencer and Francis Pratt bought the Slater Mill lot and water rights in 1865, and operated a spinning factory for the next thirty years. This operation was one of the last textile firms in the Slater Mill, manufacturing cotton yarn, twines, and threads. The executors of Job Spencer's estate eventually sold the mill to S. Willard Thayer for the Old Slater Mill Association in 1920. (Courtesy of The Spaulding House Research Library.)

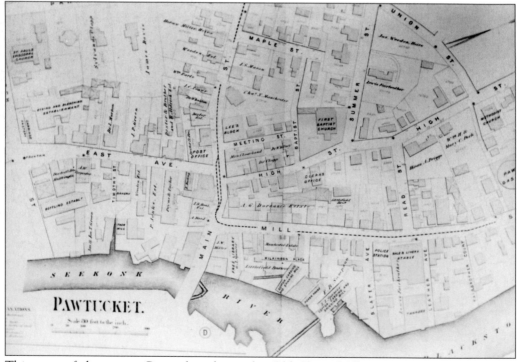

This map of downtown Pawtucket shows the Old Slater Mill as a spinning mill run by J.L. Spencer. Mill Street, parallel to the river, was home to many mills in the nineteenth century but was renamed to honor President Franklin D. Roosevelt in the 1940s. Present on this map are several spinning mills and a bleachery, as well as the churches, library, bakery, and post office that indicate a thriving town.

28

The Slater Mill building was part of an industrial community that was well established by 1870. The Wilkinson Mill is above and to the left of the Old Slater Mill. Museum architects would use this photograph in the 1970s to recreate Wilkinson Mill's cupola.

In this *c.* 1870 image, the former home of Almy, Brown, and Slater carries a sign for Nathan P. Hicks and Co., producers of ring travelers and other small machine parts. Ring travelers were U-shaped guides used on ring-spinning machines, invented by John Thorp of Providence in 1828. The traveler guided the yarn around a ring, introducing a twist.

This photograph from the Division Street Bridge illustrates the industrial landscape of the city. Mills and churches dominate the built environment, but the Blackstone River is the center of attention. Note the boats in the river below Pawtucket Falls, indicating access to Providence and the sea.

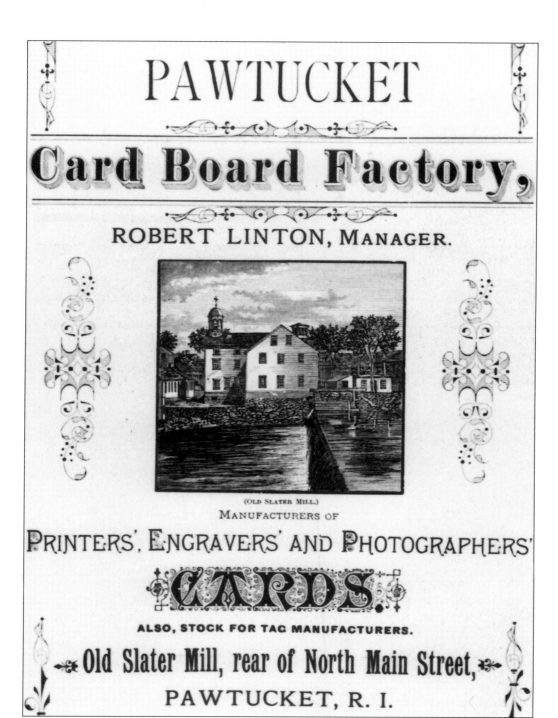

PAWTUCKET

Card Board Factory,

ROBERT LINTON, MANAGER.

(OLD SLATER MILL.)

MANUFACTURERS OF

PRINTERS', ENGRAVERS' AND PHOTOGRAPHERS'

CARDS.

ALSO, STOCK FOR TAG MANUFACTURERS.

Old Slater Mill, rear of North Main Street,

PAWTUCKET, R. I.

This ornate advertisement for the Pawtucket Cardboard Factory appeared in an 1881 edition of *Picturesque Rhode Island*, a book of essays and sketches glorifying the various cities and towns of the state. The advertisements in the book emphasize the great number of businesses in Rhode Island in the 1880s, a golden period for New England industry.

H.L. Spencer, who would run his bicycle shop out of the Old Slater Mill building in the 1890s, painted this view of the mill in 1881. Spencer used the mill as the subject for many artworks, including a series of pastels. By the time he moved his business into the building he was familiar with its symbolic appeal.

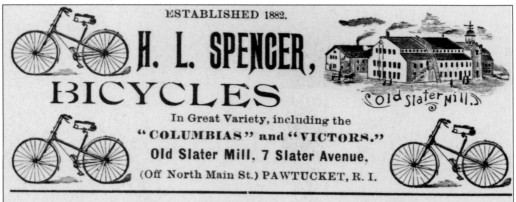

ESTABLISHED 1882.

H. L. SPENCER,

BICYCLES

(Old Slater Mill.)

In Great Variety, including the
"COLUMBIAS" and "VICTORS."
Old Slater Mill, 7 Slater Avenue,
(Off North Main St.) PAWTUCKET, R. I.

During the week of the "Cotton Centenary" the question was asked by many, where do you have your Laundry done? The answer was:

THE TROY LAUNDRY

is the place where we have our work done. It is the best Laundry in the State. Try them, and you will stay with them.

MERITHEW & KINNEY, Proprietors.

In 1890 the city of Pawtucket published an extensive program for the Cotton Centennial Celebration which included a history of the city and its prominent citizens. This advertisement for H.L. Spencer's bicycle shop depicted the Slater Mill as an active place of business with smoke coming out of its chimney.

The dam seen here was first constructed in 1792, and has been rebuilt several times due to early sabotage and general disrepair. At the time of this photograph, about 1870, the water was directed behind the Slater Mill through a raceway. The vast power of the river brought many mills to its banks, including the Pawtucket Nail Manufactory, the third building below the Slater Mill.

In 1890 the Slater Mill housed five different businesses: Pratt and Spencer (spinning); J. Crocker and Sons (wire and sheet metal goods, coffin trimmings); Frank Frost (jewelers' tools); Henry Spencer (bike sales); and Samuel Cope (files). All of this activity necessitated further growth to the building. The remains of the N.P. Hicks sign are evident from the river side.

The water rushes by in this photograph of a freshet at the Blackstone River about 1890. High water like this would disturb production up and down the river, since each mill depended on a steady flow of water into each wheel pit. Gates would be lifted and lowered, raceways filled and emptied, to account for the changes in the water. Seasonal variation was to be expected, but major flooding or drought could be a disaster.

This 1890 photograph was taken during a flood of the river. The people and horses are crossing the Main Street Bridge over the falls, which have swelled in the rain. Slater Mill can be seen behind the bridge in this image.

Joseph Rushworth peers between the shoulders of two older workers in a spinning room around 1905. The machinery is run by leather belting attached to the power system, probably a turbine. This system of line shafting and leather belts continued to be used in mills, especially the older buildings, through the mid-twentieth century.

This postcard depicts the mills next to the Slater Mill, each one dependent on the water that seems low in this image. The dormer on the Slater Mill roof was built to accommodate the needs of one of the many businesses operating within the building by this time.

The Pawtucket Hair Cloth Company used the Old Slater Mill in the 1860s, but soon discovered the building was too small for its operation. This image of the new factory in 1890 is evidence of one of Slater Mill's successes in launching new businesses in Pawtucket. Haircloth, made from horses' tails on special looms, was extremely popular in the nineteenth century for fancy chair cushions.

This birds-eye view of Pawtucket was included in a collection of images of Rhode Island industrial cities in 1904. Pawtucket was not the largest industrial city by this time, but it was still an important site of many manufacturing concerns, which provided thousands of factory jobs.

The businesses in Slater Mill were part of a thriving industrial community at the turn of the century. This photograph of the banks of the Blackstone River across from Slater Mill depicts the many factories on the other side of the dam. The waterfront would be cleared completely in the 1960s, the buildings by then abandoned and neglected.

SPAULDING HOUSE PUBLICATIONS
THE JOSEPH SPAULDING HOUSE
30 FRUIT STREET, PAWTUCKET, RHODE ISLAND 02860

BRENNAN RUG

Brennan Rug Works: Tag

This tag from Thomas J. Brennan's rug weaving shop is a rare extant piece of a product made in Slater Mill. Brennan's use of the name "Old Slater Mill" on the label is testimony to the historical prestige of the building. T.J. Brennan became involved in the carpet trade in 1893, opened his rug shop at the Slater Mill in 1904, and was among the last businesses to leave in 1923. (Courtesy of The Spaulding House Research Library.)

This postcard is one of many sold over the years depicting the Old Slater Mill. Whether used for industry or tourism, the mill has been a recognizable symbol of Pawtucket. The Pawtucket Steamboat Company, seen here, shared the mill with approximately twenty other businesses between 1900 and 1923. The company produced at least one steam car at Slater Mill.

This is a rare photograph of the interior of the Slater Mill from the beginning of the twentieth century. It shows several braiding machines and a stove for heating the workspace. Note the writing on the overhead beams warning workers not to "spit on the ceiling." The man on the left is J. Andrews, founder of Pawtucket Standard Braid, which occupied the Old Slater Mill from 1912 to 1921.

The American bicycle-riding craze of the 1890s found its way into Slater Mill by way of H.L. Spencer's bicycle-riding rink and store. In this photograph it appears Spencer sold the bikes out of the next-door building, and had his patrons practice their skills in the "Bicycle

Riding Rink" in the Slater Mill. The historic building's name had been painted on the roof, probably making it visible to passers-by on the Main Street Bridge.

This oil painting was done in 1891 by C.F. Delaney, a relative of Lyons Delaney, a prominent Pawtucket resident who owned a coffee and spice mill. This view of the upper falls was a popular subject for artists. The painting was given to the Old Slater Mill Association in 1952, as the museum prepared to open.

This small token, good for one cup of coffee, was produced by the Lyons Delaney Company, which used both the Slater Mill and the Wilkinson Mill around 1913. Coffee grinding, although much different from cotton spinning, could use the same power source and therefore the same mill. With a healthy and diversified industrial economy, the mill building had endless possibilities.

The word "Slater" has been obscured by the elevator, but this photograph clearly identifies pride in the history of the old mill. With no business signs on the front of the building, "Old Slater Mill" is the only identification this structure needs. The fire hydrant kept close by the adjacent mill was a constant reminder of the danger of fire in wooden shops.

This photograph, taken about 1900, shows High Street from Main Street. The first house on the right was built about 1775 and was owned and occupied by Samuel Slater in 1800. A century later it was the "Hotel Canada and Cafe Francais," serving the French-Canadian immigrant community. Notice the narrowness of the street and the sidewalks; this road would later be widened.

The elevator device on the front of the building in the 1920s indicates activity on the second two floors in the enlarged mill. Three business signs appear on the front of the structure, including one for a machine shop. Note the "1793" plaque on the overhang above the elevator. The line shafting that connected the water power from the Slater Mill with the building next door can be clearly seen here, to the left.

Stacy Tolman painted this mural of the Slater Mill in the auditorium at the new Tolman High School in Pawtucket in 1926. Only a few blocks away from the mill, the high school used its image to represent the city. Interestingly, Tolman chose to paint the mill in its pre-restored state, even though by 1926 the building had changed considerably.

Three

Restoration and Quiet Times

Before the restoration was to begin in 1924, Sydney Strickland of the Boston architectural firm of Strickland, Blodget and Law took several photographs of the mill and the surrounding structures. These images provide valuable information about the changes in the structure of the mill both inside and out. Strickland photographed the entire area and not just the Slater Mill; his series therefore provides an important record of the mill's surroundings, which were quite run-down by 1924.

Faced with a wooden building that had straddled a waterway for over one hundred years, the Old Slater Mill Association had to make major structural changes. They removed additions, re-built the gable roof which had been damaged by fire, and put in new windows.

Although several Pawtucket business executives had been energized by the prospect of saving the mill and sustained the project, it was difficult to raise support for the museum during periods of depression and war. In 1949, several years before the organization would hire a curator and open the museum, Providence photographer Laurence E. Tilley documented the changes that had taken place during the decades after the mill was restored.

OLD SLATER MILL, PAWTUCKET, RHODE ISLAND
FIRST COTTON MILL IN AMERICA, EST. 1790

ROBERT AMORY   STUART CRAMER   ALFRED M. COATS
JAMES R. MACCOLL   H. NELSON SLATER   ELLISON A. SMYTH
R. H. I. GODDARD   HENRY D. SHARPE   HENRY FORD
WILLIAM M. BUTLER   W. E. BEATTIE   HENRY C. DEXTER
HENRY F. LIPPITT, ROBERT R. JENKS AND OTHERS

recognizing that the establishing in 1790 by Samuel Slater of the first cotton mill in this country was one of the most important factors in the industrial progress and prosperity of the United States have the honor of inviting

Mr. John F. Street

to join with them in acquiring this first cotton mill and converting it into a

NATIONAL TEXTILE MUSEUM

where shall be gathered and preserved an historical exhibit of the cotton industry from its beginning to the present time.

It is also most fitting that this mill should be made a permanent memorial to the founders and the present leaders of the cotton industry

This 1920s fund-raising letter was addressed to John F. Street, whose grandson Henry would be elected president of the Old Slater Mill Association in 1962. The association used the names of well-known manufacturers such as Henry Ford and H.N. Slater (of Slater & Sons) to encourage support on a national level; however, raising money from the national textile firms proved almost impossible. This image has been touched up to remove surrounding mill buildings which were still part of the landscape in 1920.

The first president of the Old Slater Mill Association, Henry Dexter was a tireless advocate for saving and restoring the mill. He traveled widely in the 1920s, attending conferences to raise money for the museum. Textile executives like Dexter made up the board of the Old Slater Mill Association for many decades. There was a strong connection between the museum and the industry, which still had a base in Rhode Island.

This view down Slater Avenue shows several buildings which have since been torn down. The house on the left was Samuel Slater's house for several years. The Slater Mill is the building at the end of the road. A flat roof had been installed after a serious fire in 1912. (Courtesy of Freeman, Brigham and Hussey, Ltd.)

Samuel Slater's house was a meat market in 1924. Although there had been talk of saving the house as well as the mill, interestingly it was the factory building that survived. This was a departure from the traditional model of historic preservation which concentrated on the places famous people slept, rather than where they worked. (Courtesy of Freeman, Brigham and Hussey, Ltd.)

Although this street had changed considerably since the mid-nineteenth century, these houses are still recognizable as mill housing for the many factories in the area. Cities up and down the Blackstone River still have row houses such as these, built at the same time and close to the mill where the residents would work.

The end of Slater Avenue in the 1920s was an industrial center, bordered by mills. The Slater Mill is on the far left, with the Wilkinson Mill behind it. Towering smokestacks and chimneys, as well as a streetlight, indicate the use of the area, although most of these buildings would be torn down in the next few years. (Courtesy of Freeman, Brigham and Hussey, Ltd.)

In the 1920s the Slater Mill had many additions, including this toilet tower. Most of these extra structures would be removed in the massive restoration of 1924–25. The building that had expanded to fit the needs of various businesses and different owners would be restored according to the ideas of the Old Slater Mill Association. (Courtesy of Freeman, Brigham and Hussey, Ltd.)

The front of the building prior to restoration needed a lot of work. The paint, elevator, and roof all showed massive wear, and without the Old Slater Mill Association, the mill may have fallen into even greater disrepair. By 1924 the last tenants, Pawtucket Electro-Plating and the Moncrief Machine Company, had vacated the premises and the architects prepared to begin the long process of restoration. (Courtesy of Freeman, Brigham and Hussey, Ltd.)

This close-up depicts the cupola during restoration. Although the original mill of 1793 probably did not have a cupola and bell, the Slater Mill did have a cupola by 1812. Many area mills would have had bells, all competing to call their employees to work. (Courtesy of Freeman, Brigham and Hussey, Ltd.)

In this image the mill has not yet been "taken back" to its 1835 appearance. The left side of the building still includes a massive addition, which would be removed, since museum architects wanted to scale back the size of the greatly expanded mill. Although the renovations would take the building back in time, the mill was not restored to the time of Samuel Slater, perhaps because the end result would have been too small for a new museum, and because of a lack of evidence about the specifications of the original 1793 building. (Courtesy of Freeman, Brigham and Hussey, Ltd.)

During the restoration of 1924–25, the interior of the mill was cleaned and completely stripped of machinery, undoubtedly a daunting task. Multiple windows on each side provided light, but the mill had also been wired for electricity. This photograph shows the vast space that had once housed dozens of businesses but was now ready for museum exhibits.

Soon after the restoration, visitors from all over the country began to arrive. In this photograph, delegates from the Virginia Chamber of Commerce pose in front of the renovated historic structure. The mill had been radically altered, and all parts of it had been rebuilt, including the fenestration.

In 1928 Slater Mill was the site of a ceremony honoring the 100th anniversary of the invention of ring spinning. John Thorp revolutionized spinning with the introduction of this improvement, which increased the rate at which yarn could be spun.

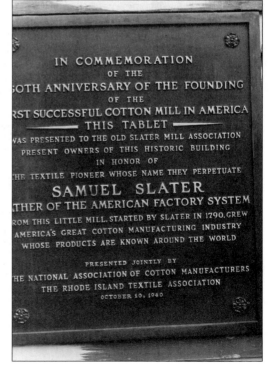

In 1940, Slater Mill was honored by the National Association of Cotton Manufacturers and received this plaque which still decorates the front of the building. Before the mill had opened as a museum, the Old Slater Mill Association struggled to get attention and support from both the local and national cotton industry.

In 1944 the Blackstone Valley Electric Company restored the dam next to the Slater Mill. The dam was first built in July of 1792 by Oziel Wilkinson and Almy, Brown, and Slater, owners of the property and water rights. Although the dam inspired admiration, it also created resentment, since the construction diminished available water power at the main falls downstream. (Courtesy of Blackstone Valley Electric Company.)

When a dam is made of earth, stone, and wood, it will deteriorate. In this photograph from 1944, workers have made forms over the existing structure, and will pour concrete to make a more permanent repair. Aside from a wooden sluice gate, the repair stands unchanged. (Courtesy of Blackstone Valley Electric Company.)

The interior of the mill in 1949 was set up to host trade shows, with partitions for each display and a stage on the left. The machinery in the mill when this photograph was taken does not appear to relate specifically to the textile industry, and the permanent exhibit had not yet been set up.

This view of the tower end of the first floor shows the original 1793 part of the mill. The restoration replaced many structural components, but some of the beams and cornerposts remain.

In this wintry scene, the full extent of the restoration's demolition of the industrial landscape is evident. None of the buildings which surrounded the Slater Mill are still standing. The association trimmed the area directly around the building, and put up the fence, but for the 1940s the rest of the space was left empty.

Pawtucket was defined by the river, as other cities are by natural formations of coal or other ores. This city's factory-based economy was dependent on the relevance of water power. Slater Mill Dam, once fought over and treasured, was left behind as the twentieth century found new sources of power and built new industrial cities.

Laurence E. Tilley of Providence took photographs of all sides of the mill in 1949, as well as several interior shots. These invaluable photographs are among the only images of the mill from the 1940s, since this was a period of general inactivity at the site. (Courtesy of Laurence E. Tilley.)

Laurence E. Tilley took this photograph of the back of the Slater Mill in 1940. The fence line curves around the Slater Avenue end, indicating that the association had landscaped and planted the entire front section of the property, leaving the river side boarded up and unfinished. (Courtesy of Laurence E. Tilley.)

In this Tilley photograph of the garret, the structure of the old charred roof can be seen clearly, along with the addition of new pipes. The growing museum collection had already begun to fill up the storage area with machines and books. Machinery and records from area mills had been donated in anticipation of an industrial museum. (Courtesy of Laurence E. Tilley.)

Obscured by trees, the Slater Mill seems removed from its industrial heritage, the restored facade a stark contrast to its appearance only a few decades before. Trees planted during the association's landscape project in the 1920s had grown around the building in the years before it was officially opened.

The 1810 Wilkinson Mill, which would join Slater Mill as part of the historic site in 1973, was used as a furniture warehouse in the 1940s and most likely had dumped some extra products on its front lawn. Behind all the file cabinets, desks, and pews is a nice view of the newly constructed walkway to the Slater Mill. (Courtesy Laurence E. Tilley.)

Four

Museum and Community Center

The main focus of the early decades of the Old Slater Mill Association was to save the building from demolition and preserve it for future generations; the mission of the 1950s and 1960s was to keep the doors open to the public. In order to introduce Pawtucket's residents to their rich textile history, the museum staff coordinated dozens of exhibits designed to attract people to the mill. The photographs in this chapter document an active community site, with children and adults alike enjoying this cultural resource.

By painting the mill building red, the association attempted to create a different kind of environment from the industrial Pawtucket that residents saw every day. They consulted a horticulturist, who recommended lilacs as appropriate decorative plants for an eighteenth-century structure. Although these plants did not fit with the industrial history of Slater Mill, they remain around the building today.

In 1949, the Old Slater Mill Association painted the mill "New England Barn Red," trying to evoke a rustic setting even in the midst of industrial decay. Cars and parking lots take up vacant space left by the demolished mills.

The rear windows are filled with glass, showing the completed final touches of the restoration. Across the river, old factory buildings can still be seen in this photograph, although in a decade they would be torn down.

This early 1950s photograph of the first floor before any exhibits had been added includes a plaque with the names of the Old Slater Mill Association founding members.

Slater memorabilia made up much of the collection in the early years of the museum. In this photograph are Slater's violin, a quilt made by his second wife, Esther, and a nail said to be from the original mill. The collection also includes a trunk Samuel Slater supposedly carried from England and a swatch of fabric from his church pew.

The second floor of the museum stored extra machines in the 1950s, some of which would be conserved and added to the permanent exhibit of cotton machinery downstairs.

This publicity shot for the opening of the museum in 1955 shows off the tourist-friendly components of the new setting for Slater Mill. The pole for the raising of the American flag has a prominent place here, and the new museum sign beckons to passers-by.

Daniel Tower was the first curator of the Old Slater Mill, hired by H. Nelson Slater in 1952. He researched and wrote a history of the mill, and created and built the first permanent exhibit. Tower's decision to open the museum to the public in 1955 went against the wishes of Nelson Slater, who thought the museum would never survive if it opened too early. Unfortunately, Tower never lived to prove Slater wrong. He died at the age of forty in 1956.

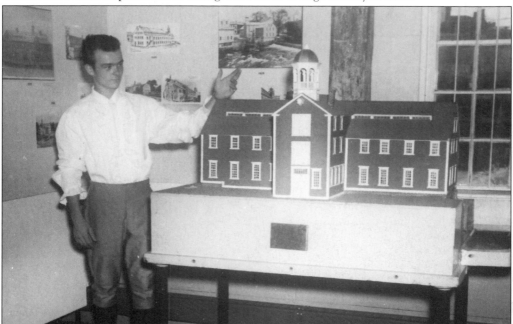

Jim Briden, one of the museum's first tour guides, poses with a model of the Slater Mill. The model, painted red along with the mill in 1949, was commissioned by H. Nelson Slater and built by local woodworker Seth Albert Yates in 1930. Briden was dressed in knickers and buckled shoes, probably because the museum wanted to illustrate the "colonial" origins of the mill.

This photograph, taken to show damage from the 1955 flood, is one of the only images of the first permanent exhibit. A portrait of Samuel Slater hangs on the left, and a late-nineteenth-century painting of the mill is on the right. On the center panels are images of the early cotton industry: the words "THE STORY OF SAMUEL SLATER" are reflected in the water.

Although it did not cause extensive damage, the flood of 1955 was troublesome for the new, under-funded museum.

Hannah Wilkinson stares into the eyes of her soon-to-be-husband Samuel Slater in this 1955 ABC production of *Slater's Dream*. This made-for-TV movie, emphasizing the legend of Slater's secretive flight to America and his financial triumphs with Moses Brown, was shown for many years to visitors at the Slater Mill as an introduction to the tour. (Courtesy of E.I. du Pont de Nemours and Company.)

This unusual night view shows the lit-up mill perhaps glowing for a special event. The addition of the words "Open Daily" to the museum sign evidence the early success of the site as a community resource that Pawtucket residents returned to again and again.

The adaptation of the mill building to suit tourists and schoolchildren included blocking off part of the second floor for a theater. Many museum tours begin with a film to orient visitors to the site: this audience is watching *Slater's Dream*, a dramatization of the romance and intrigue of the beginnings of the industrial revolution.

Donald Shepard, the second director of the mill, presents an award to the Pawtucket Junior Women's Club in 1957. The close association between service organizations and the museum was important in the early years of the museum. The women's clubs raised money for the mill, purchasing, among other things, chairs for meetings and presentations and a kitchen stove for receptions.

Local women's groups, such as the Pawtucket Garden Club, helped the museum in many capacities in the 1950s and 60s. Pictured here is their herb garden, which complemented the hand-spinning and weaving demonstrations by showcasing over fifty herbs and plants. This extensive garden, affectionately named "Industry in Bloom," opened in 1958.

Now a thriving museum, the Slater Mill looked out on the bricked-up New York Furniture Company's warehouse. Once an important place for innovation in the machine tool industry, the Wilkinson Mill was now a furniture warehouse. The building was saved despite the mass destruction of other industrial structures.

H. Nelson Slater, John Nicholas Brown, and Norman MacColl, members of the Old Slater Mill Association, stand in the first-floor exhibit in 1958. MacColl had been president of Lorraine Manufacturing, a major factory complex which closed in 1954, selling off an extensive array of buildings and machinery. As textile mills continued to leave Rhode Island, the industry had less of an official connection with the Slater Mill museum.

Director Donald Shepard took some schoolchildren around the mill in the 1950s. While the upstairs exhibits brought the crowds on the weekends, school tours made up the basis of the daily visitation.

Miss Maid of Cotton 1955 stands in a cotton dress on her visit to Slater Mill, a requisite stop for state beauty pageant winners in the 1950s and '60s. She showcases here the model of Samuel Slater's carding frame, built for the museum before its opening. The original machine is at the Smithsonian Institution in Washington, D.C.

This picturesque photograph of the mill reflected in the Blackstone also shows the rebuilt stone wall on the river end of the building. During the 1950s, the Old Slater Mill Association continued to improve the area around the mill.

Members of the Old Slater Mill Association Board of Trustees sit amidst old wooden beams at a meeting in 1962. Women had been allowed on the board only five years earlier. In the front row at the left of the photograph is Henry Street, elected during this meeting to the presidency of the board.

These girls, finalists in the local Little Miss Maid of Cotton contest of 1963, vied to represent Rhode Island against seventeen other cotton-producing or manufacturing states. Although most cotton mills had left Rhode Island by this time, the state was still a symbolic part of the national cotton community throughout the 1960s. (Courtesy of *The Pawtucket Times*.)

Inside the mill, visitors could view the vast array of machinery that had been donated to the museum from other area mills. Much of the machinery still in the museum today was made in Pawtucket, Central Falls, Providence, or Worcester. This Crane Knitting Machine, donated to the mill in 1960, made tubes of seamless fabric for use in sweatshirts, tee-shirts, and linings.

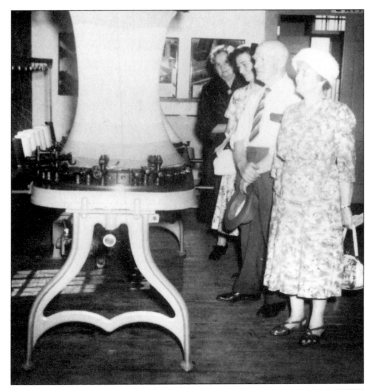

As part of the celebration of Pawtucket's Diamond Jubilee in 1961, local women dressed in historic costumes and took tea on the grounds of the Slater Mill. The 75th anniversary of the incorporation of the city of Pawtucket took place in a city searching for a new identity. Slater Mill, recently opened as a museum, was an important centerpiece of the rejuvenation of the city.

Maude Crabbs spun flax, as shown here, and other fibers for the museum in the 1960s. While demonstrating weaving, she produced place mats and cloth napkins, which sold in the gift shop. Behind her in this photograph are other tools for the hand-production of flax into linen, including the scutching board to her left.

These girls, visitors to a glass exhibit in 1962, point to one of the panels set up on the second floor. This exhibit was sponsored by the National Early American Glass Club, insuring an automatic audience for the historic mill. By collaborating with other museums and other clubs, Slater Mill could introduce different parts of the community to textile history.

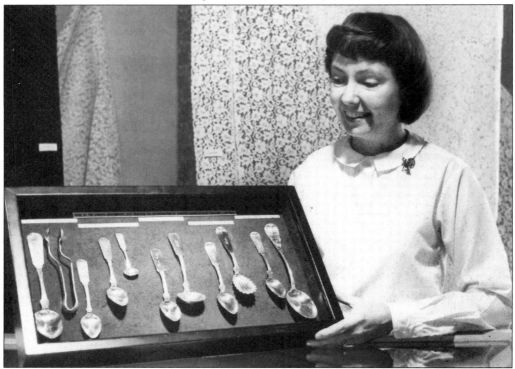

Betty Johnson coordinated many successful exhibits like the 1962 "Sterling on Lace." This exhibit highlighted two local industries and was one of the eleven yearly shows the museum hosted in order to bring people in the doors.

Trade fairs, in which local businesses displayed their tools and machinery, helped build awareness about the various industries present in Rhode Island. These boys visited the museum in 1964 and examined the New England Machine and Electric presentation. The ubiquitous pegboard behind them was a versatile exhibit technique, used to mount dozens of exhibits in the 1960s.

Exhibits of new techniques and chemical processes evidenced an important industrial optimism during the Trade Fair of 1964. Slater Mill, a place of historic innovation and technological expertise, was an ideal site at which to showcase local industry.

The Junior Women's Club held an annual book fair on the second floor of the museum. Events like this one, in 1961, helped raise enthusiasm for the mill by encouraging people with different interests to come through the doors and see the museum and its textile exhibits.

One of the benefits of a tour at Slater Mill are the demonstrations of textile machinery, unusual even in industrial museums. Children, who would visit with school groups during the week and then bring their parents back for free weekend tours, helped the museum build support in the community.

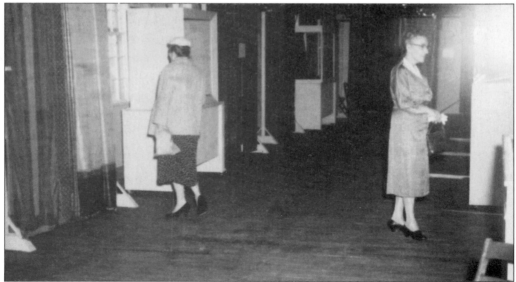

Although the exhibit program of the 1960s was not limited to textile-related topics, exhibits of rugs, quilts, and other textiles always brought in visitors. Craft shows and displays by the Pawtucket Art Club also helped to bring in the community.

Five
Urban Renewal and Site Expansion

The Slater Mill has stood for over two hundred years in the same spot on the banks of the Blackstone, and photographs of the site provide a unique record of Pawtucket's history. The photographs in this chapter illustrate the significant changes in the site as urban renewal transformed the landscape and the museum expanded to include new buildings and new stories.

Construction work for the urban renewal project in the 1960s temporarily limited visitation at the Slater Mill, as dozens of buildings on Roosevelt Avenue and Main Street were destroyed. The end result of the project was an unobstructed view of the mill from surrounding streets. Also, by tearing down adjacent mills, the city cleared the way for Hodgson Rotary Park, landscaped next to the Wilkinson Mill in 1970.

When Almy, Brown, and Slater built their mill in 1793, it was a promise of a new way of life; when urban renewal cleared the area, the mill was left standing as evidence of an era gone by. Recreated environments at Slater Mill Historic Site teach visitors about craft production, industrial innovation, and historic preservation.

These two photographs emphasize the destruction of Pawtucket which took place during urban renewal and the building of Interstate 95. The photograph above was taken in the 1950s, and shows the newly landscaped Slater Mill grounds. Across the river are factories, houses, smokestacks, and billboards, all advertising an active industrial town. In the photograph below, taken in 1973 to celebrate the newly created Slater Mill Historic Site, the area across the river has been completely transformed. Parking lots and an Apex shopping center replaced historic buildings, and the highway cuts through neighborhoods at the top of the image.

The construction of Hodgson Rotary Park was an important undertaking for the Slater Mill museum, since it finalized the era of industrialization in the area, giving over the entire grounds to city beautification and tourism. A $50,000 donation by Percy Hodgson of the city's Rotary Club funded the creation of the park, celebrated here at the ground-breaking ceremony in 1970.

For decades, the Wilkinson Mill was used for furniture storage. While factories had been built with windows on both sides to let the light in, this was unimportant to a warehouse and the windows had been bricked over. One of the first projects in the restoration was to replace the windows, restoring the historic facade.

Interstate 95 destroyed many eighteenth- and nineteenth-century houses in its path through Rhode Island in 1962. This one was saved because of its legendary connection to Samuel Slater, who slept there in 1790. The house had to be moved through the city, and brought to the parking lot of the Slater Mill museum, where it was safe from demolition. (Courtesy of *The Pawtucket Times*.)

The Sylvanus Brown House sat unused for a decade, but was finally incorporated into Slater Mill Historic Site in 1972. A new foundation and basement kitchen were entirely rebuilt for the house in its new location.

Research into the original color of the mill prompted director Patrick Malone to call for the repainting of the building in 1975. Although period paintings showed the mill to have been yellow as early as 1812, most Pawtucket residents in the 1970s had grown accustomed to the red color and lamented the drastic change.

The Wilkinson Mill and the Sylvanus Brown House joined the Slater Mill to form the newly designated "Slater Mill Historic Site" in 1973. Much work was needed on both of these buildings. The Sylvanus Brown House required new clapboards, paint, and roofing, as well as a completely rebuilt lower floor. The Wilkinson Mill was only a shell in this photograph. Local artisans and masons rebuilt the stone end of the building.

As part of the restoration project, the Wilkinson Mill received a new cupola. Through the enlargement of a nineteenth-century photograph of the mill, the original structure of this building was revealed and could be recreated. The bell came from a demolished textile mill in Fall River, Massachusetts.

The interior of the Wilkinson Mill has been recreated to look like a machine shop from the middle to late 1800s. All machines came from area mills which had closed down, and the leather belting was donated by the Crown and Eagle Mills in Uxbridge, Massachusetts. Machine shops, which fix and build other machines, would have been prevalent in a city like Pawtucket, with many mills that needed attention.

Several excavations in the 1970s provided information used to construct and operate a new waterwheel by 1980. While at first the water had to be pumped in by electricity, the following year archaeologists found the raceway from the Blackstone River under the Wilkinson Mill. Water flowing from the river through the raceway turned the mid-breast wheel again in 1982.

The first floor of the Slater Mill was filled with working machinery in the 1970s, demonstrating the transformation from cotton plant to cotton cloth. Seen here on the left is the Draper Loom (1892), a machine that turned out yards and yards of plain cotton sheeting and shirting in cotton mills all over New England.

Curators furnished the interior of the Sylvanus Brown House to look like an artisan's house of the early nineteenth century. Brown was a pattern-maker who worked for Samuel Slater when he first arrived in Pawtucket. The house is used in the tour to discuss hand-production of wool and flax.

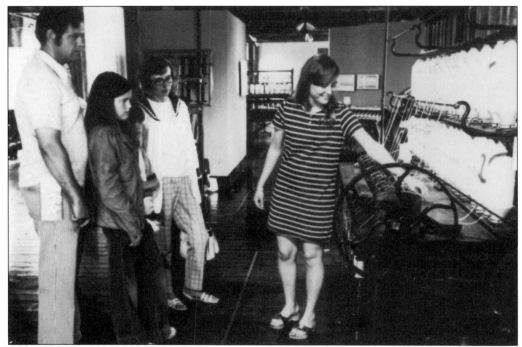

This 1970s tour guide shows visitors the late-nineteenth-century spinning frame, which puts the final twist onto the cotton yarn. As most of the textile industry had left New England by the 1970s, fewer and fewer visitors were familiar with the historic machinery.

Behind the center post in this photograph, the permanent exhibit stands ready for visitors. Using the space for a museum instead of a mill meant adding spotlights to the ceiling beams, instead of relying on kerosene lamps and window light as the mill workers did.

One of the most popular festivals on the site is the annual Labor and Ethnic Heritage Festival, which celebrates the communities the textile industry brought to the Blackstone Valley. Here, folk singers entertain a crowd in front of the Slater Mill in 1990.

A child watches as a sheep is shorn during a program called "Sheep to Shawl" on the grounds in 1990. Nearby, another demonstrator will wash and card the wool, and a spinning wheel and loom will finish the process.

These third-floor roof beams were numbered in 1793 to insure proper fit. Recorded by the Historic American Engineering Record in 1991, these beams help explain how the mill was originally constructed. (Courtesy of Joseph E.B. Elliott, photographer, Historic American Engineering Record of the National Park Service, United States Department of the Interior.)

The attic storage at Slater Mill houses a collection of equipment and old artifacts, nails, boxes, and spools of yarn. This image shows the construction of the roof. (Courtesy of Joseph E.B. Elliott, photographer, Historic American Engineering Record of the National Park Service, United States Department of the Interior.)

This painting continues the tradition of artists using Slater Mill as a subject. David Macauley, an illustrator who has served on the board of the Old Slater Mill Association, painted this image in 1990 to commemorate two hundred years of spinning by water power. (Courtesy of David Macauley.)

To commemorate the 200th anniversary of the signing of the Constitution, each of the original thirteen colonies issued a postage stamp. Slater Mill represents Rhode Island on its stamp, celebrating the importance of the building to the state and to America. The stamp ceremony in Pawtucket drew crowds to Slater Mill Historic Site.

The Slater Mill as it stands in the 1990s is a composite of many peoples' visions and hopes. Its shape today is a melange of eras, industries, and tourists who have come together to create the Slater Mill.

The turbines under the Slater Mill are not now being used actively to power machinery, but they were used in the Slater Mill until the twentieth century. Although the machinery in the mill is now run by electricity, the presence of these turbines, still lying under the mill, help historians uncover the story of water power. (Courtesy of Joseph E.B. Elliott, photographer, Historic American Engineering Record of the National Park Service, United States Department of the Interior.)

This birds-eye view of the Slater Mill and environs was taken as part of a study by the Historic American Engineering Report in conjunction with the National Park Service. This project documented historic industrial buildings all over the country, creating a valuable national archive. (Courtesy of Joseph E.B. Elliott, photographer, Historic American Engineering Record of the National Park Service, United States Department of the Interior.)

This 1995 photograph of the site by Salvatore Mancini showcases the power of the water at Pawtucket Falls. Indeed, the Blackstone River is the most important component of the successful industrial communities that grew around its banks. (Courtesy Salvatore Mancini.)